Preface

In the ever-evolving landscape of computer science, a strong command over data structures and file organization is essential for designing efficient, reliable, and scalable software systems. These concepts form the backbone of algorithm development and memory management, making them critical for students and professionals alike. To support learners in mastering these foundational topics, **"IGNOU BCA Data and File Structure Previous Year Unsolved Papers MCS 021"** offers a thoughtfully curated collection of unsolved question papers from previous IGNOU examinations.

This book is designed to encourage deep conceptual understanding and promote independent problem-solving. The questions span a wide array of topics including arrays, linked lists, stacks, queues, trees, graphs, hashing techniques, and file organization methods such as sequential, indexed, and direct access. Presented in an unsolved format, these papers challenge students to apply theoretical knowledge to practical problems, strengthening analytical skills and boosting exam preparedness. We hope this resource becomes a trusted companion in your academic journey, equipping you with the tools needed to succeed in both assessments and real-world computing challenges.

Table of Contents

Preface.. 1
Chapter 1: Term-End Examination, June- 2014 3
Chapter 2: Term-End Examination, December- 2014 5
Chapter 3: Term-End Examination, June- 2015 7
Chapter 4: Term-End Examination, December- 2015 8
Chapter 5: Term-End Examination, June- 2016 9
Chapter 6: Term-End Examination, December- 2016 10
Chapter 7: Term-End Examination, June- 2017 12
Chapter 8: Term-End Examination, December- 2017 14
Chapter 9: Term-End Examination, June- 2018 15
Chapter 10: Term-End Examination, December- 2018 17
Chapter 11: Term-End Examination, June- 2019 19
Chapter 12: Term-End Examination, December- 2019 21
Chapter 13: Term-End Examination, June- 2020 24
Chapter 14: Term-End Examination, February- 2020 26
Chapter 15: Term-End Examination, June- 2021 28
Chapter 16: Term-End Examination, December- 2021 30
Chapter 17: Term-End Examination, June- 2022 32
Chapter 18: Term-End Examination, December- 2022 34
Chapter 19: Term-End Examination, June- 2023 36
Chapter 20: Term-End Examination, December- 2023 38

MCS – 021
M. C. A. (REVISED)/B. C. A. (REVISED)
(MCA/BCA)

Chapter 1: Term-End Examination, June- 2014

MCS-021: DATA AND FILE STRUCTURES

Time: 3 Hours
Maximum Marks:100
Weightage: 75%

Note: (i) Question No. 1 is compulsory.
(ii) Answer any three Questions from the rest.
(iii) All algorithms should be written near to C language.

1. (a) Prove by induction that` 10
   (i) The number of leaves in a binary tree of height 'h' are less than or equal to 2h.
   (ii) The number of nodes in a full binary tree of height 'h' are equal to (2h+1-1).

   (b) Write an algorithm to implement Doubly Linked List. 10

   (c) Compare Heap sort and Quick sort with each other. 10

   (d) Write an algorithm for addition of two Sparse Matrices. 10

2. (a) Write an algorithm for insertion sort. Write step by step working of the algorithm for The following set of data. 43, 16, 11, 89, 32, 46, 1, 88 10

   (b) What is a splay tree? Write the steps involved in a top-down splaying procedure. 10

3. (a) How is a circular queue better than a linear queue? Also, write functions for adding and removing an element from the circular queue. 10

   (b) Write an algorithm for implementing a singly linked list using arrays. 10

4. (a) Write prim's algorithm for constructing a minimum cost spanning tree and trace algorithm on the following network. 10

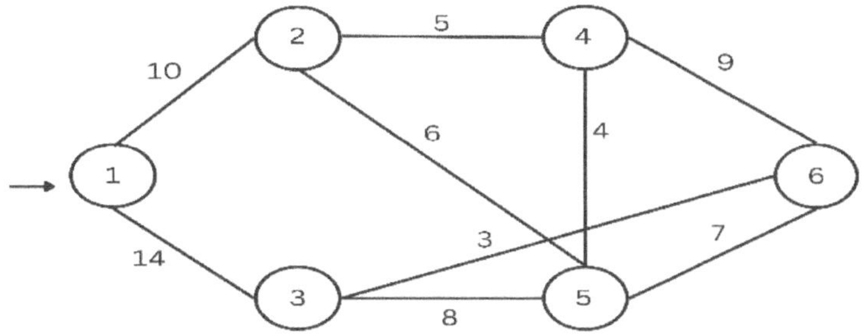

(b) Discuss the various file organisation methods. Also, list the advantages and disadvantages of each. 10

5. (a) Explain the depth first search algorithm with an example. 10

(b) What are Red-Black Trees? What is their significance ? 10

MCS – 021
M. C. A. (REVISED)/B. C. A. (REVISED)
(MCA/BCA)

Chapter 2: Term-End Examination, December- 2014

MCS-021: DATA AND FILE STRUCTURES

Time: 3 Hours
Maximum Marks: 100
Weightage: 75%

Note: (i) Question No. 1 is compulsory.
(ii) Answer any three Questions from the rest.
(iii) All algorithms should be written near to C language.

1. (a) Consider the algorithm given below : 10
(i) scanf ("%d", &n);
(ii) (for (int i = n; i<=n*n; i = n + 10)
(iii) (for (int j = 1; j <= n; j++)
(iv) printf ("%d", n/i + j);}}
Calculate the complexity (both space and time) of the above code by using Big "O" notation.

(b) Define sparse matrix. Write an algorithm that accepts a 6x5 sparse matrix and outputs in 3- tuple representation. 10

(c)Write an algorithm for Heapsort. Write step by step working of algorithm for the following set of data: 9, 16, 43, 27, 91, 33, 21, 7, 3 10

(d) Draw AVL tree by inserting the following elements one by one: 7, 13, 27, 9, 11, 14, 8, 37, 24 10

2. (a) Write Floyd-Warshall's algorithm computing "All pair shortest path" Show how does your algorithm work for the following graph: 10

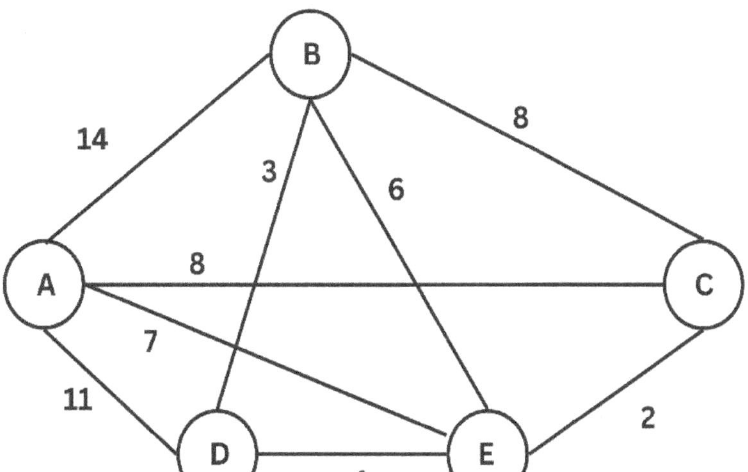

(b) Write an algorithm for inserting a node in a Red-Black tree. Write step by step working of algorithm using an example. 10

3. (a) Write an algorithm for adding two polynomials. Algorithm should take the two Polynomials as input and display the resultant polynomial. 10

(b)Write an algorithm for array implementation of a circular queue. 10

4. (a) Write an algorithm to insert and delete a node from a doubly-linked list. 10

(b) Write an algorithm to insert an element into a B-tree. Make B-tree using your algorithm for the following list elements: 22, 29, 8, 34, 17, 89, 11, 19 10

5. (a) Compare any two file organisations. 10

(b) What is a BST? Explain with an example. What are its limitations? 10

MCS – 021
M. C. A. (REVISED)/B. C. A. (REVISED)
(MCA/BCA)

Chapter 3: Term-End Examination, June- 2015

MCS-021: DATA AND FILE STRUCTURES

Time: 3 Hours
Maximum Marks: 100
Weightage: 75%

Note: (i) Question No. 1 is compulsory.
(ii) Answer any three Questions from the rest.
(iii) All algorithms should be written near to C language.

1. (a) Describe the asymptotic notations in detail. 10

(b) Write an algorithm to implement the insertion and deletion operations into a singly linked list. 10

(c) What is a circular queue? Write an algorithm for insertion and deletion in a circular queue. 10

(d) Explain the types of rotations performed on AVL trees with an example. 10

2. (a) Write an algorithm to perform each of the following operations: 10
(i) Insertion of an element into a linear array.
(ii) Delete every third element from a linear array.
(b) Write an algorithm to implement dequeue using array. 10

3. (a) Define binary tree. What are the traversals in binary tree? Explain each traversal with an example. 10

(b) Create a Binary Search Tree for the following alphabets. Start from an empty BST.
R, F, G, B, Z, U, P, K, L. Show the trees at each stage. 10

4. (a)Discuss the Prim's algorithm to find the minimum cost spanning tree. 10

(b) Explain the process of converting a tree to a binary tree. 10

5. (a) Illustrate inserting an element into a heap with the following numbers:
2,3,81,62,1,20,35,15,9,48. 10

(b) Write a short note on various file organizations. 10

MCS – 021
M. C. A. (REVISED)/B. C. A. (REVISED)
(MCA/BCA)

Chapter 4: Term-End Examination, December- 2015

MCS-021: DATA AND FILE STRUCTURES

Time: 3 Hours
Maximum Marks: 100
Weightage: 75%

Note: (i) Question No. 1 is compulsory.
(ii) Answer any three Questions from the rest.
(iii) All algorithms should be written near to C language.

1. (a) Write an algorithm that accepts two polynomials as input and prints the resultant polynomial due to the addition of input polynomials. 10

   (b) What is a stack? Explain the various operations of stack with an example for each operation. 10

   (c) Write an algorithm for each of the following: 10
   (i) Depth first search
   (ii) Breadth first search

   (d) What is a Splay Tree? How does it differ from a Tree? 10

2. (a) Write an algorithm for the implementation of a doubly linked list. 10

   (b) Write an algorithm for the implementation of a stack. 10

3. (a) Write a non-recursive algorithm for inorder traversal of a binary tree. 10

   (b) Define B-tree. Give an example of a B-tree. 10

4. (a) Explain Kruskal's algorithm with an example. 10

   (b) What are red-black trees? Explain the properties of a red-black tree. 10

5. (a) Explain QuickSort algorithm. Trace the algorithm for the following set of data:
   25, 0,8, 78, 6, 34, 56, 90, 100 10

   (b) Explain the merits and demerits of various file organisations. 10

MCS – 021
M. C. A. (REVISED)/B. C. A. (REVISED)
(MCA/BCA)

Chapter 5: Term-End Examination, June- 2016

MCS-021: DATA AND FILE STRUCTURES

Time: 3 Hours
Maximum Marks: 100
Weightage: 75%

Note: (i) Question No. 1 is compulsory.
(ii) Answer any three Questions from the rest.
(iii) All algorithms should be written near to C language.

1. (a) Define "Time Complexity" and "Space Complexity". What are the differences between them? 10

(b) Write the algorithms for inserting and deleting elements in a singly linked list. 10

(c) Write an algorithm to implement a stack, using arrays. 10

(d) Explain various operations performed in a B-tree. 10

2. (a) What is a Sparse Matrix ? What are the advantages and disadvantages of Sparse Matrix representation? 10

(b) What is a circular queue? Explain how it can be implemented using arrays. 10

3. (a) Draw a binary search tree (BST) for the input 8, 14, 23, 18, 38, 45, 56, 82, 70. Trace the algorithm to insert the node 20 into the BST. 10

(b) Define "AVL Tree". Write any two applications of AVL Trees. 10

4. (a) What is DFS? What is BFS? Explain the differences between them. 10

(b) Explain Dijkstra's algorithm with an example. 10

5. (a) Illustrate inserting an element into a heap with the following numbers: 2, 3, 81, 64, 4, 25, 36, 16, 9, 49 10

(b) Compare and contrast the Splay trees with AA trees. 10

MCS – 021
M. C. A. (REVISED)/B. C. A. (REVISED)
(MCA/BCA)

Chapter 6: Term-End Examination, December- 2016

MCS-021: DATA AND FILE STRUCTURES

Time: 3 Hours
Maximum Marks: 100
Weightage: 75%

Note: (i) Question No. 1 is compulsory.
(ii) Answer any three Questions from the rest.
(iii) All algorithms should be written near to C language.

1. (a) Write an algorithm for multiplication of two matrices. 5

(b) Find the order of the function 3n + 2. 5

(c) Write an algorithm to add two polynomials. 10

(d) Write the recursive algorithm for various tree traversals. Trace your algorithm for the following data of a Binary Tree: 1, 2, 3, 4, 5, 6, 7, 8, 9, 10, 11, 12 10

(e) What is a red-black tree? Explain the properties of a red-black tree with an example. 10

2. (a) Write the algorithms for various operations performed on a circular linked list. 10

(b) Explain the advantages and disadvantages of a Circularly Linked List over a Singly Linked List. 10

3. (a) What are the merits and demerits of using pointers over arrays? Explain. 10

(b) What are the different operations that can be performed on a stack? Explain with examples. 10

4. (a) Explain any two rotations performed on an AVL tree with examples. 10

(b) What is meant by minimum cost spanning tree? Apply Kruskal's algorithm to find the minimum cost spanning tree of the following graph: 10

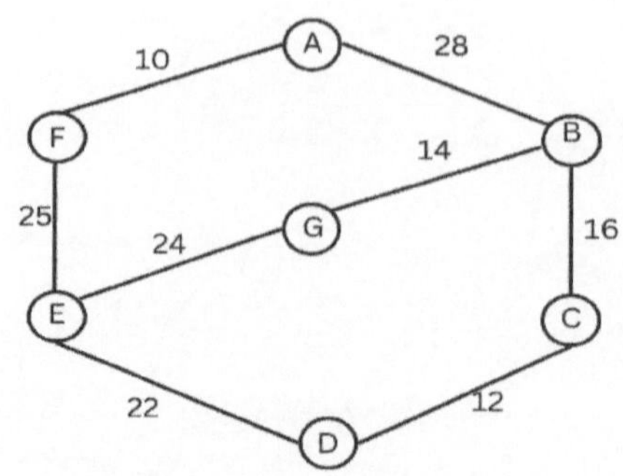

5. (a) Write an algorithm for quick sort. Trace the algorithm for the following set of data:
25, 0, 8, 78, 6, 34, 56, 90, 100 10

(b) Compare and contrast linear search and binary search. 10

MCS – 021
M. C. A. (REVISED)/B. C. A. (REVISED)
(MCA/BCA)

Chapter 7: Term-End Examination, June- 2017

MCS-021: DATA AND FILE STRUCTURES

Time: 3 Hours
Maximum Marks: 100
Weightage: 75%

Note: (i) Question No. 1 is compulsory.
(ii) Answer any three Questions from the rest.
(iii) All algorithms should be written near to C language.

1. (a) Prove by induction that
   (i) the number of leaves in a Binary Tree of height 'h' are less than or equal to 2^h. 5
   (ii) the number of nodes in a full Binary Tree of height 'h' is equal to (2h+1-1). 5

   (b) Write an algorithm for Heap Sort. Write the step-by-step working of the algorithm for the following set of data:5, 25, 13, 36, 78, 95, 3, 6 10

   (c) Explain the types of rotations performed on AVL trees with an example of each. 10

   (d) Write the algorithm for each of the following:
   (i) Depth First Search 5
   (ii) Breadth First Search 5

2. (a) Write Prim's algorithm and construct a minimum cost spanning tree on the following network using Prim's algorithm: 10

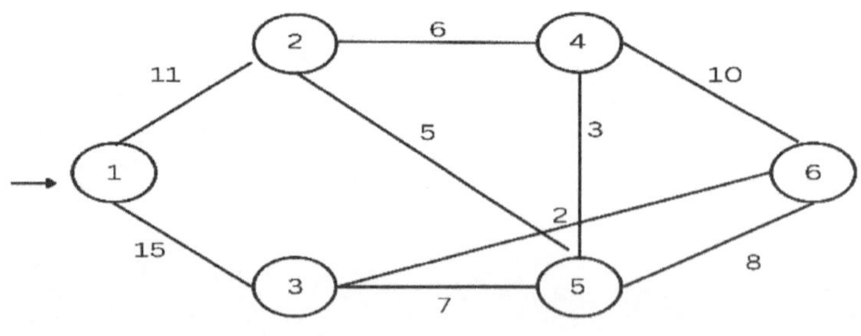

   (b) Write an algorithm for the addition of two Sparse Matrices. 10

3. (a) Write an algorithm for array implementation of a Circular Queue. 10

   (b) Create a Binary Search Tree for the following alphabets. Start from an empty BST.
   S, U, B, D, K, V, A, L 10

4. (a) Write a non-recursive algorithm for inorder traversal of a Binary Tree. 10

(b) Explain the process of converting a Tree to a Binary Tree. 10

5. (a) Write an algorithm for the implementation of a Singly Linked List. 10

(b) Name the sorting algorithm which accepts an input string that is already sorted yet performs at its worst case to give a sorted output. Explain your answer. 10

MCS – 021
M. C. A. (REVISED)/B. C. A. (REVISED)
(MCA/BCA)

Chapter 8: Term-End Examination, December- 2017

MCS-021: DATA AND FILE STRUCTURES

Time: 3 Hours
Maximum Marks: 100
Weightage: 75%

Note: (i) Question No. 1 is compulsory.
(ii) Answer any three Questions from the rest.
(iii) All algorithms should be written near to C language.

1. (a) Write an algorithm for insertion of an element and deletion of an element from priority queue. 10

(b) Explain quick sort algorithm and determine its complexity in best case and worst case scenarios. 10

(c) Explain garbage collection and compaction methods with an example. 10

(d) What is a threaded binary tree? Explain with the help of examples. What are its advantages? 10

2. (a) How do you represent both stack and queue using a one-dimensional array? 10

(b) Generate a binary tree by traversing inorder and preorder sequences given below: 10
Inorder: B, E, D, A, G, F, H, C
Preorder: A, B, D, E, C, F, G, H

3. (a) Change the following infix expression into postfix expression: A-B(CD-E)^F/G 10

(b) Write a C program for inserting a new node at the end of a doubly linked list. Write its time complexity. 10

4. (a) Explain the memory representation of a lower triangular matrix. Determine the address formula of any element aij $1 \leq i \leq n$ in the lower triangular matrix if the elements are stored in row major order. 10

(b) Write a C program to add two polynomials using a single variable. 10

5. (a) What is an AVL tree? Explain the balancing methods of an AVL tree with an example 10

(b)(i) Define Hash function. Explain collision resolution strategies. 5
(ii) What is a Sparse Matrix? How do you represent a sparse matrix ? 5

MCS – 021
M. C. A. (REVISED)/B. C. A. (REVISED)
(MCA/BCA)

Chapter 9: Term-End Examination, June- 2018

MCS-021: DATA AND FILE STRUCTURES

Time: 3 Hours
Maximum Marks: 100
Weightage: 75%

Note: (i) Question No. 1 is compulsory.
(ii) Answer any three Questions from the rest.
(iii) All algorithms should be written near to C language.

1. (a) What is data structure? Explain different types of data structures with examples. 10

(b) Write an algorithm for adding an element to a circular queue and removing an element from a circular queue using arrays. 10

(c) Write an algorithm for converting the following infix expression into postfix expression using a stack: A+(B*C-(D/E^F) *G) * H 10

(d) (i) What is asymptotic notation? Explain the big 'O' notation. 5
(ii) Explain three different applications of stacks with the help of examples. 5

2. Write the function to implement recursive version of pre-order, in-order and post-order traversals of Binary trees. 20

3. (a) Draw Binary search tree that results from inserting into an initially empty tree record with keys given below in order: E, A, S, Y, Q, U, E, S, T, I, O, N and then deleting Q. 10

(b) Write a program in `` C " to insert and delete elements from a circular queue using a linked list. 10

4. (a) (i) Compare any two different sorting techniques. 5
(ii) How does static allocation differ from dynamic allocation of memory? 5

(b) (i) Find the incidence matrix of the following graph:

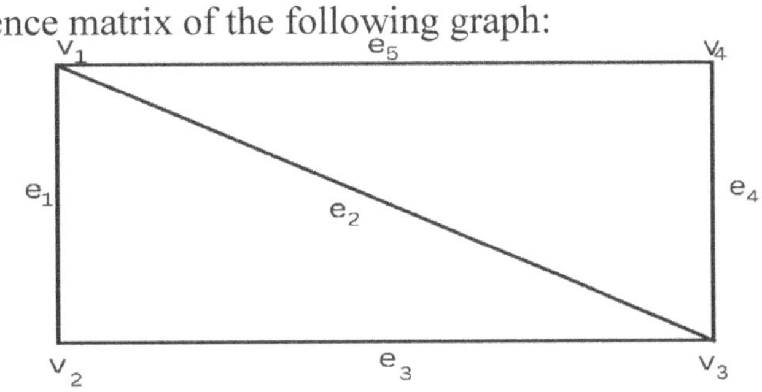

(ii) Draw all non-similar trees with exactly six nodes. 5

5. Write short notes on the following: 4×5=20

(a) AVL Tree

(b) Priority Queue

(c) Operation on Stack

(d) Hash Function

MCS – 021
M. C. A. (REVISED)/B. C. A. (REVISED)
(MCA/BCA)

Chapter 10: Term-End Examination, December- 2018

MCS-021: DATA AND FILE STRUCTURES

Time: 3 Hours
Maximum Marks: 100
Weightage: 75%

Note: (i) Question No. 1 is compulsory.
(ii) Answer any three Questions from the rest.
(iii) All algorithms should be written near to C language.

1. (a) Describe big O notation and Ω notation. 10

(b) Explain the process of converting a tree into a binary tree. 10

(c) Write an algorithm to implement stack, using array. 10

(d) What is linear search? Write linear search algorithm and find its time complexity. 10

2. (a) What is sparse matrix? Explain 3-tuple representation of a sparse matrix with the help of an example. 10

(b) Explain Indexed Organization. Sequential 10

3. (a) Write an algorithm for creation of a circular queue and deletion of an element from a circular queue. 10

(b) Traverse the following binary tree in Pre-order and Post-order. 10

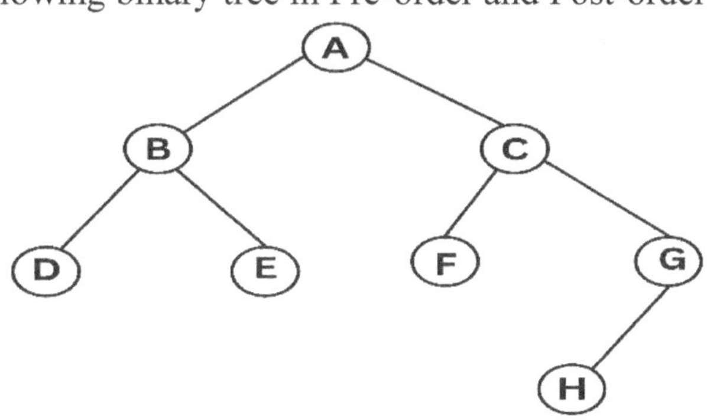

4. (a) Explain inserting an element into a heap with the following numbers:
4, 5, 21, 18, 16, 64, 2 10

(b) Find Minimum Cost Spanning Tree (MCST) of the following graph using Prim's algorithm. Show all the intermediate steps. 10

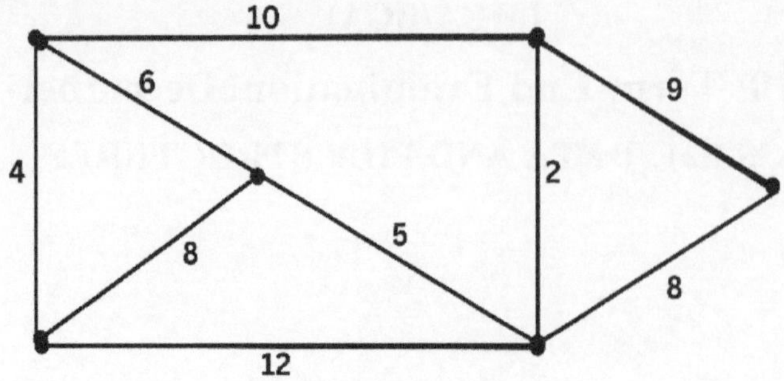

5. (a) Sort the following set of data using Insertion sort: 25,15, 10, 18, 12, 4, 17 10

(b) Write algorithms for the following: 10

(i) Inserting element in a doubly linked list.

(ii) Deleting element from a doubly linked list.

MCS – 021
M. C. A. (REVISED)/B. C. A. (REVISED)
(MCA/BCA)

Chapter 11: Term-End Examination, June- 2019

MCS-021: DATA AND FILE STRUCTURES

Time: 3 Hours
Maximum Marks: 100
Weightage: 75%

Note: (i) Question No. 1 is compulsory.
(ii) Answer any three Questions from the rest.
(iii) All algorithms should be written near to C language.

1. (a) Order the following functions by their complexity in increasing order: 3
   (i) n!
   (ii) 3
   (iii) $\sqrt{n}$
   (iv) log2 (n!)

(b) For the function defined by f(x) = 2x3 + 4x + 1, show that f(x) = 0 (x^3) using the definition of O (big Oh). 4

(c) Convert the following prefix notation into infix notation: + -*** ABCD/E/F + GH 3

(d) Write an algorithm to reverse a string using a stack. Illustrate all the intermediate steps of your algorithm on the string "IGNOU". 6

(e) Use Kruskal's algorithm to construct a minimum cost spanning tree of the following graph: 6

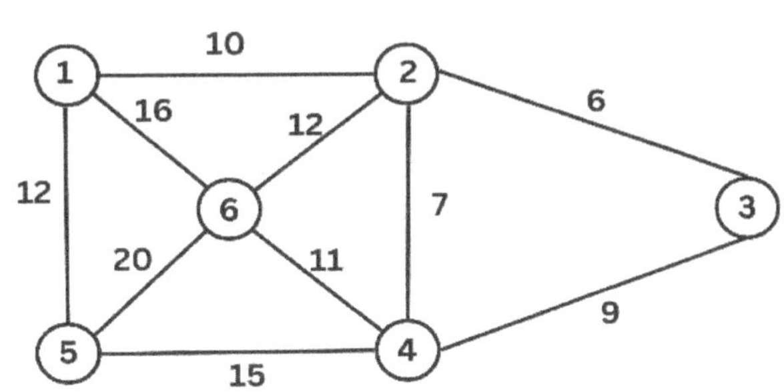

(f) Apply 2-way mergesort for sorting the following numbers and show all the intermediate steps: 4 6 3 7 1 9 2 8 5 6

(g) Insert the following data items into a B-Tree of order 5:
a b e h p c k d m l n u t x y 6

(h) Explain how a polynomial can be represented using an array. Write an algorithm to add two polynomials. 6

2. (a) Write an algorithm to do insertion sort and analyze its run-time complexity. 10

(b) Write a program that accepts a set of integers and creates a singly linked list of these integers. Then it should prompt for input of an integer and delete the node consisting of that integer from the singly linked list. 10

3. (a) Write a recursive algorithm of preorder and inorder traversal of a binary tree and explain it. 10

(b) What is a strongly connected component of a graph? Write an algorithm for finding strongly connected components of a graph. 10

4. (a) Explain Floyd-Warshall's all pair shortest path algorithm. How is it different from single source shortest path? 10

(b) Given the input file (5, 10, 15, 8, 20, 16, 28, 35, 55, 40, 30), construct IGNOU

(i) A binary tree 3

(ii) Heap 4

(c) Draw the graph corresponding to the following adjacency matrix:

	a	b	c	d
a	0	1	1	0
b	1	0	0	1
c	1	0	0	1
d	0	1	1	0

5. (a) Construct an AA-tree using the following numbers (nodes). Show all the intermediate steps and balancing of tree. 7 14 21 80 4 50 30 40 10

(b) Write important properties of:

10

(i) Binary search tree

(ii) Red black tree

MCS – 021
M. C. A. (REVISED)/B. C. A. (REVISED)
(MCA/BCA)

Chapter 12: Term-End Examination, December- 2019

MCS-021: DATA AND FILE STRUCTURES

Time: 3 Hours
Maximum Marks: 100
Weightage: 75%

Note: (i) Question No. 1 is compulsory.
(ii) Answer any three Questions from the rest.
(iii) All algorithms should be written near to C language.

1. (a) Order the following functions by their complexity in increasing order: 3
(i) n log n
(ii) (log n)2
(iii) 3n2+7n
(iv) 4n

(b) Given the function f(x)=3x3−2x2+1 , show that f(x)=O(x^3) using the definition of O (big oh). 4

(c) A recursive function is given below: 6
f(int x){if (x < 2) return 1 else return f(x - 1) + f(x - 2)}
What is the value of f(5)f(5)f(5)? Show a complete recursion tree.

(d) Evaluate the postfix expression:623 + - 382 / + * 2 * * 3 +

(e) How do you define balance of a subtree? Construct an AVL-tree (height-balanced tree) for the following sequences of input:j a d n o s m f j k l

(f) Apply the Bubble sort algorithm to sort the following list. What is the time complexity of Bubble sort?35 30 10 40 25 28 15 9 8

(g) Apply Dijkstra's single-source shortest path algorithm to find out the shortest path from vertex 'a' to every other vertex of the following graph: 8

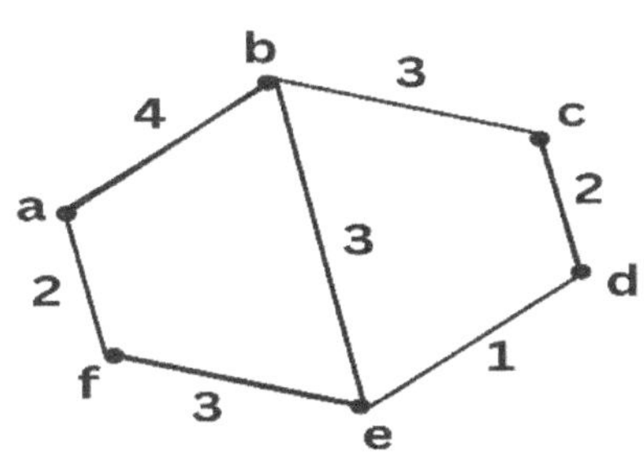

2. (a) Write an algorithm for Greatest Common Divisor (GCD) of the two integers m and n. Also, calculate the best case and the worst-case time complexity of the algorithm. 10

(b) Write an algorithm to implement a stack through a linked list and delete an item from it. 10

3. (a) Write an algorithm to implement a Depth First Search method. Write the order of node sequences it will visit in the following graph using V1 as the source vertex: 10

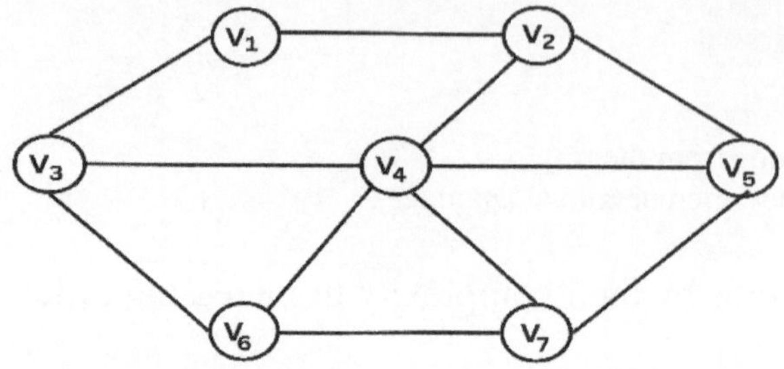

(b) Make a 3-tuple representation of non-zero elements of the following 6 x 5 sparse matrix: 3

	1	2	3	4
0	0	4	0	0
1	0	3	0	1
2	0	0	5	0
3	0	0	2	1
4	0	0	6	0
5	0	0	5	4

(c) Write an algorithm to implement a circular array and explain the logic. 7

4. (a) What is a minimum spanning tree? Apply Prim's algorithm to find the minimum spanning tree of the following graph: 10

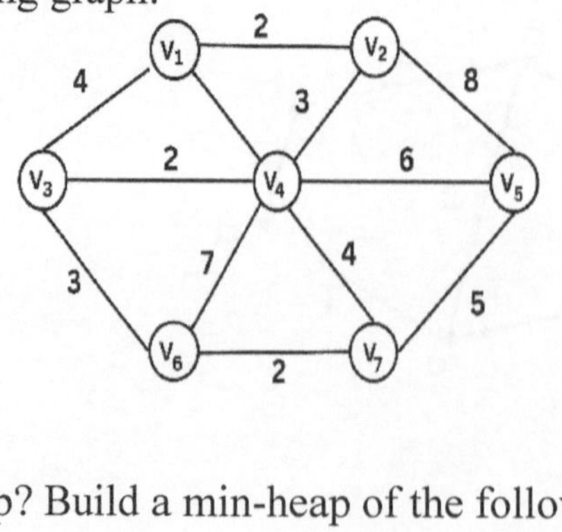

(b) What is a min-heap? Build a min-heap of the following sequences using a top-down approach: 10

5. (a) What are the properties of a Red-Black Tree (RBT)? Explain the process of inserting a node into an RBT through an example. 10

(b) Given the following Binary Search Tree (BST), write down its preorder and postorder traversal schemes: 6

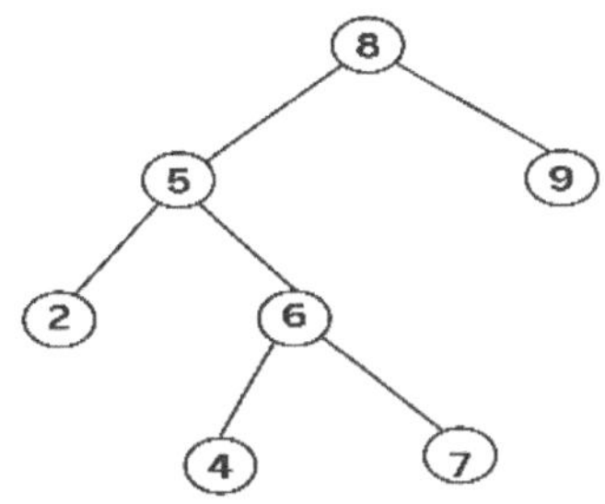

(c) Explain the following terms: 4

(i) Asymptotic Analysis

(ii) Indexed Sequential File

MCS – 021
M. C. A. (REVISED)/B. C. A. (REVISED)
(MCA/BCA)

Chapter 13: Term-End Examination, June- 2020

MCS-021: DATA AND FILE STRUCTURES

Time: 3 Hours
Maximum Marks: 100
Weightage: 75%

Note: (i) Question No. 1 is compulsory.
(ii) Answer any three Questions from the rest.
(iii) All algorithms should be written near to C language.

1. (a) Write linear/sequential search algorithm and calculate time and space complexity of it. 10

(b) Write an algorithm for linked list to: 10
(i) Insert an element after a given element.
(ii) Delete an element after searching it in the list.

(c) What is splay tree? How is it different from a tree? Explain. 10

(d) Explain any two rotations performed on an AVL tree with the help of an example. 10

2. (a) Write an algorithm which takes a matrix as input and displays 3-tuple representation of the matrix. 10

(b) What is binary tree? Write non-recursive pre-order binary tree traversal algorithm. 10

3. (a) Write adjacency list and adjacency matrix representation of the following graph: 10

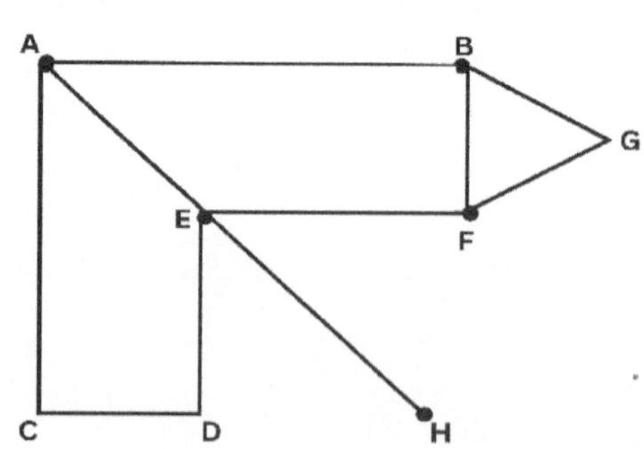

(b) What is the need of file organization? Explain division-remainder hashing with the help of an example. 10

4. (a) Sort the following list using bubble sort algorithm. Show intermediate steps of sorting:
5, 18, 29, 6, 22, 8, 1 10

(b) Explain Depth First Search (DFS) with the help of algorithm. Also, tell the time complexity of DFS. 10

5. (a) What is B-Tree? Explain the structure of B-Tree. Write B-Tree search algorithm. 10

(b) What is circular queue? List any two applications of circular queue. Write an algorithm to delete a given element from a circular queue. 10

MCS – 021
M. C. A. (REVISED)/B. C. A. (REVISED)
(MCA/BCA)

Chapter 14: Term-End Examination, February- 2020

MCS-021: DATA AND FILE STRUCTURES

Time: 3 Hours
Maximum Marks: 100
Weightage: 75%

Note: (i) Question No. 1 is compulsory.
(ii) Answer any three Questions from the rest.
(iii) All algorithms should be written near to C language.

1. (a) Write 'C' program to implement queue using array. 10

(b) Write binary search algorithm. Find its time complexity. Explain the process of finding 10 in the following list using binary search. 2 6 8 10 12 15 10

(c) Write quick sort algorithm and sort the following list using quick sort algorithm. Show intermediate steps of sorting.16 8 12 9 6 2 5 10

(d) Traverse the following tree in Preorder and Postorder. 10

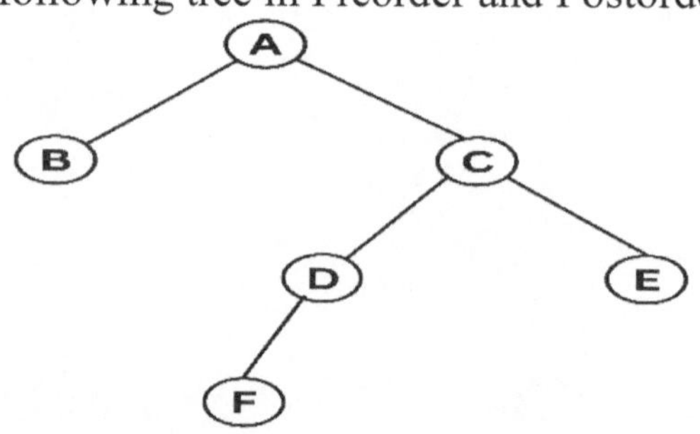

2. (a) Write Dijkstra's Algorithm for finding the shortest path. 10

(b) Write push and pop functions for stack data structure using a linked list. 10

3. (a) Write an algorithm to add two polynomials. 10

(b) Convert the following infix expression into postfix expression: 10
(A + B) * (C / D) - E

4. (a) Find the minimum cost spanning tree for the following graph using Prim's Algorithm. 10

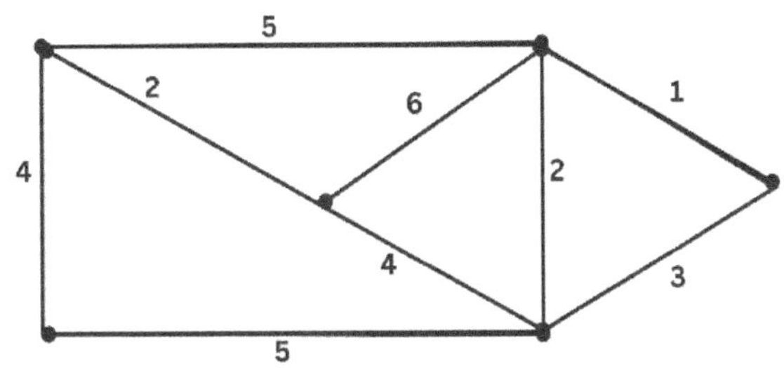

(b) What is sequential file organization? What are its disadvantages? Explain how indexed sequential file organization is better than sequential file organization. 10

5. (a) Write an algorithm for inserting a node in a Red-Black tree and explain it with the help of an example. 10

(b) Explain the structure of a binary tree. Write an algorithm for the implementation of a binary tree. 10

MCS – 021
M. C. A. (REVISED)/B. C. A. (REVISED)
(MCA/BCA)

Chapter 15: Term-End Examination, June- 2021

MCS-021: DATA AND FILE STRUCTURES

Time: 3 Hours
Maximum Marks: 100
Weightage: 75%

Note: (i) Question No. 1 is compulsory.
(ii) Answer any three Questions from the rest.
(iii) All algorithms should be written near to C language.

1. (a) Write an algorithm for push and pop operations of a stack. Also, write an algorithm to check whether the stack is empty or not. 10

(b) What is a circular queue? Write algorithms for adding an element to and deleting an element from a circular queue. 10

(c) Describe Big O and Ω notations in detail. 10

(d) Find the minimum cost spanning tree for the graph given below using Kruskal's algorithm. 10

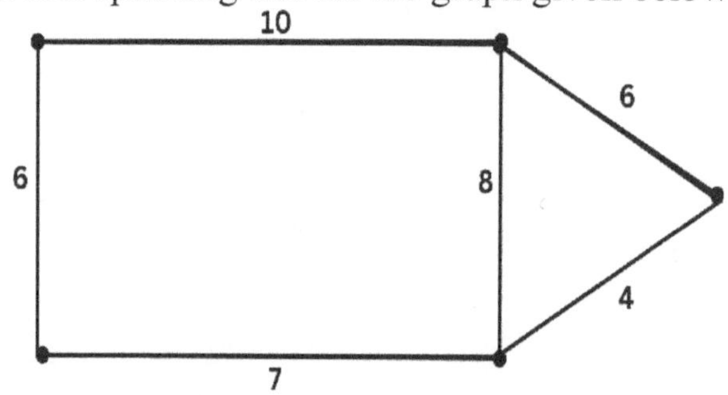

2. (a) What is an AVL tree? Explain how a node is inserted into an AVL tree and how a node is deleted from an AVL tree. 10

(b) Write any five differences between arrays and pointers in the 'C' Programming Language. 5

(c) Write a linear search algorithm and find its time complexity. 5

3. (a) What is a Red-Black Tree? Explain its properties. 6

(b) Explain Direct-File organization. 6

(c) Sort the following list using bubble sort in ascending order:25, 29, 8, 68, 92, 30, 40 Show intermediate steps of the process. 8

4. (a) Traverse the following Binary tree in:

(i) Pre-order

(ii) Post-order 10

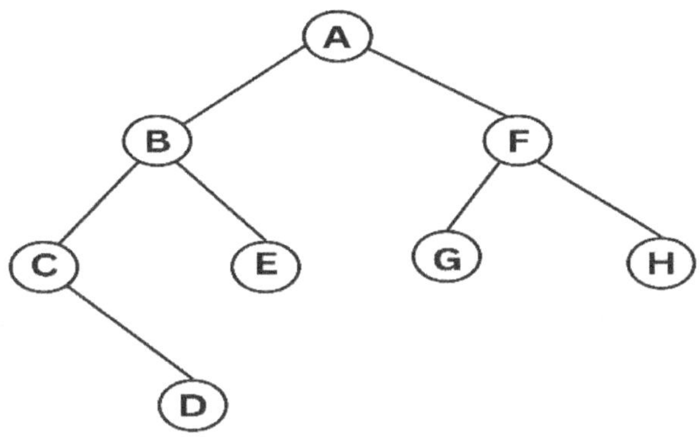

(b) Write an algorithm to implement a singly linked list using pointers. 10

5. (a) Explain the difference between row-major representation of an array and column-major representation of an array with the help of a suitable example. 10

(b) Write short notes on the following: 5

(i) Adjacency matrix representation of graph

(ii) Binary search

Chapter 16: Term-End Examination, December- 2021

MCS-021: DATA AND FILE STRUCTURES

Time: 3 Hours
Maximum Marks: 100
Weightage: 75%

Note: (i) Question No. 1 is compulsory.
(ii) Answer any three Questions from the rest.
(iii) All algorithms should be written near to C language.

1. (a) What is a sparse matrix? Explain 3-tuple representation of a sparse matrix with the help of a suitable example. 10

(b) Write the process for converting the following infix expression into a postfix expression using a stack: X ∗ Y ∗ (Z | P – Q) ∗ T + R 10

(c) Find the Adjacency Matrix for the following graph: 5

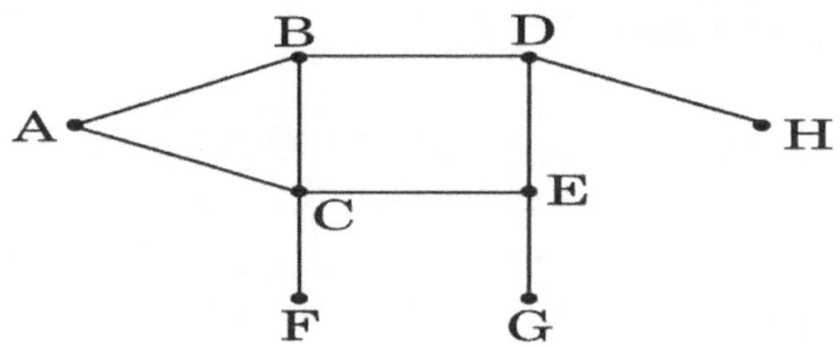

(d) Write an algorithm to create a doubly-linked list and add elements to it. 5

(e) Find the minimum cost spanning tree for the following graph using Prim's algorithm. Show all the intermediate steps of the process. 10

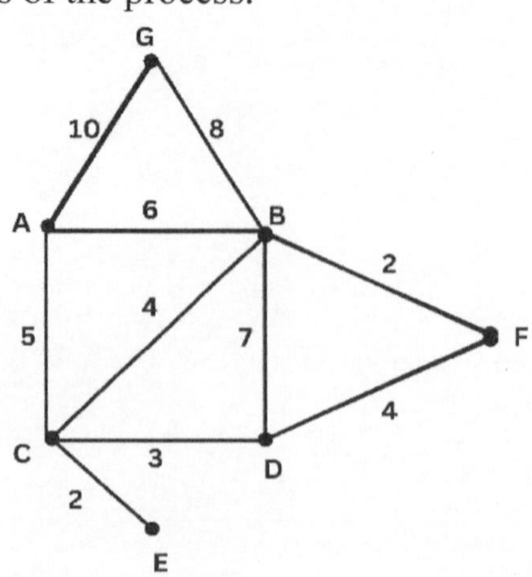

2. (a) Write the Depth First Search (DFS) algorithm and traverse the following graph using the DFS algorithm: 10

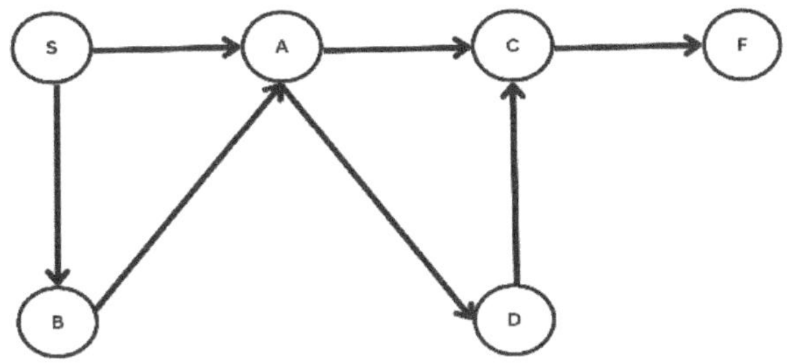

(b) Explain Indexed Sequential File organization with the help of an example. Also, write its advantages. 10

3. (a) Write an algorithm for the addition of two polynomials. 10

(b) What is Heap Sort? What is its complexity? Explain how a heap is created using an example. 10

4. (a) Explain how Static memory allocation is different from Dynamic memory allocation. In which situation is Static memory allocation a better choice? Explain briefly. 10

(b) Briefly explain AA-Trees. 10

5. (a) Write an algorithm to add two matrices using arrays. Also, find the time complexity of this algorithm. 10

(b) Write short notes on the following: $2 \times 5 = 10$

(i) Forest

(ii) Priority Queue

MCS – 021
M. C. A. (REVISED)/B. C. A. (REVISED)
(MCA/BCA)

Chapter 17: Term-End Examination, June- 2022

MCS-021: DATA AND FILE STRUCTURES

Time: 3 Hours
Maximum Marks: 100
Weightage: 75%

Note: (i) Question No. 1 is compulsory.
(ii) Answer any three Questions from the rest.
(iii) All algorithms should be written near to C language.

1. (a) What is an Algorithm? Explain the properties of an algorithm. Explain time complexity and space complexity of an algorithm, with the help of a suitable example. 10

(b) Write Kruskal's algorithm. For the graph given below, show the various steps involved in the construction of the Minimum Cost Spanning Tree using Kruskal's algorithm. 10

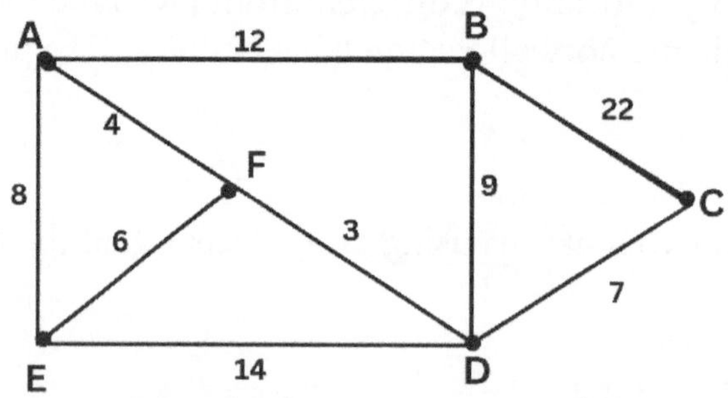

(c) Write a 'C' program for insertion and deletion of a node in a linked list. 10

(d) Write Preorder and Postorder traversal of the tree given below: 10

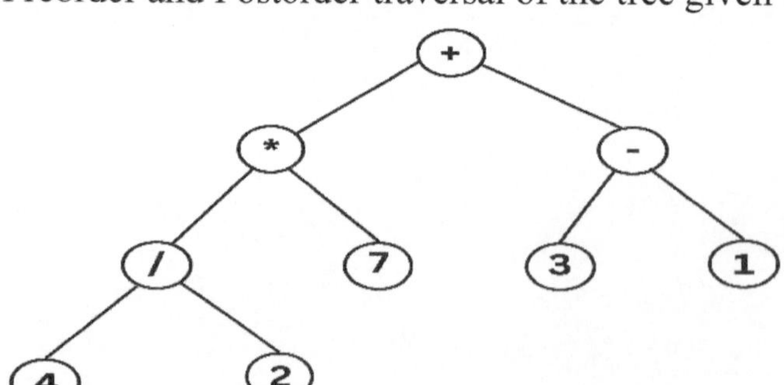

2. (a) What is Circular Queue? Write an algorithm to add an element and delete an element in a circular queue. 10

(b) Write Breadth-first search algorithm. 5

(c) Explain Direct File Organisation. 5

3. (a) Write an algorithm to check whether a stack is empty or not. 5

(b) Describe Big 'O' and 'Ω' notations. 5

(c) What is a Red-Black Tree? Explain the properties of a Red-Black Tree. 10

4. (a) Define AVL Tree. Write the algorithm to insert a node into an AVL tree and delete a node from an AVL tree. 10

(b) Write Pseudo code for Bubble Sort Algorithm. Sort the following list using bubble sort in ascending order: 35, 39, 10, 8, 78, 92, 20, 50 Also, write the steps involved. 10

5. (a) Write a program that accepts a matrix as input and prints the 3-tuple representation of it. 6

(b) Explain the Indexed Sequential File Organisation. 4

(c) What is Hashing? Explain its use. Also, explain the concept of hashing functions, with an example. 10

MCS – 021
M. C. A. (REVISED)/B. C. A. (REVISED)
(MCA/BCA)

Chapter 18: Term-End Examination, December- 2022

MCS-021: DATA AND FILE STRUCTURES

Time: 3 Hours
Maximum Marks: 100
Weightage: 75%

Note: (i) Question No. 1 is compulsory.
(ii) Answer any three Questions from the rest.
(iii) All algorithms should be written near to C language.

1. (a) Write an algorithm of 2-way Merge Sort. Also, discuss the advantages and disadvantages of 2-way Merge Sort. Also, calculate its time complexity. 10

(b) Traverse the following Binary tree in Pre-order and Post-order: 10

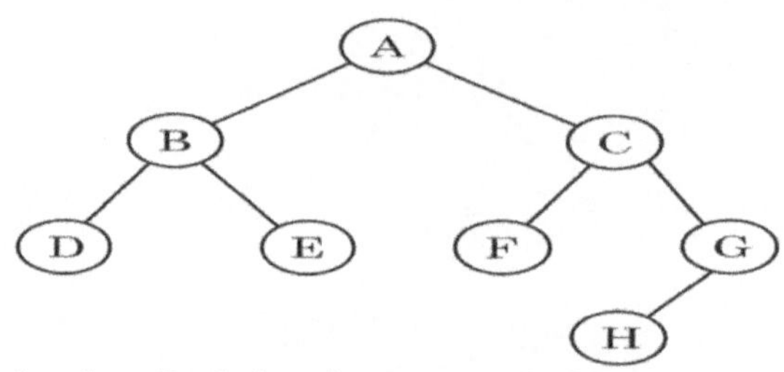

(c) Write the steps involved to find the shortest path from Vertex '1' of the graph given below by using Dijkstra's algorithm: 10

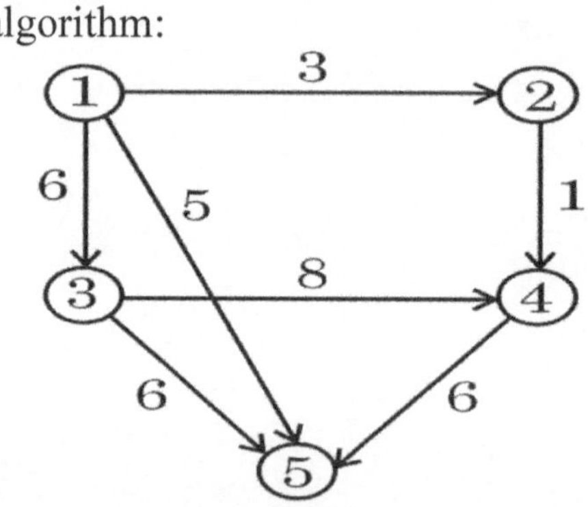

(d) Write an algorithm to implement the Depth First Search (DFS) method. Use the DFS method to traverse the following graph, with Vertex V1 as the source vertex: 10

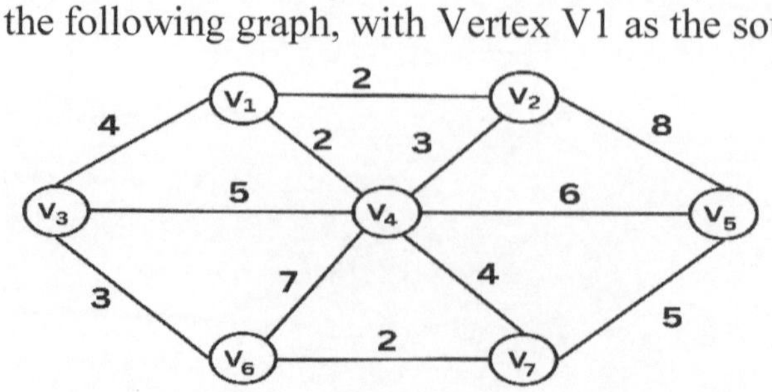

2. (a) Write short notes on the following: 10
   (i) Sequential File Organization
   (ii) Indexed Sequential File Organization

(b) Differentiate between the following: 10
   (i) Heap and Tree
   (ii) B-Tree and Binary Tree
   (iii) B-Tree and B+-Tree
   (iv) Binary Tree and Binary Search Tree

3. (a) What is a Red-Black tree? Explain its properties. 5

(b) Write an algorithm of Binary Search. 5

(c) Write the Selection Sort algorithm. Sort the following list using Selection Sort in descending order: 25, 10, 50, 21, 65, 18, 45 5

(d) Let 'E' denote the following algebraic expression: 5
[a + (b - c)] * [(d - e) / (f + g - h)] Draw the Binary tree for 'E'.

4. (a) Compute the time complexity of Bubble Sort and Quick Sort algorithms. Verify the statement "Best case for Bubble Sort is the worst case for Quick Sort." 10

(b) Write an algorithm and Pseudo code for the following: 10
   (i) Inserting an element in a doubly linked list.
   (ii) Deleting an element from a doubly linked list.

5. (a) Write Kruskal's algorithm. Find the Minimum Cost Spanning Tree of the graph given below using Kruskal's algorithm: 10

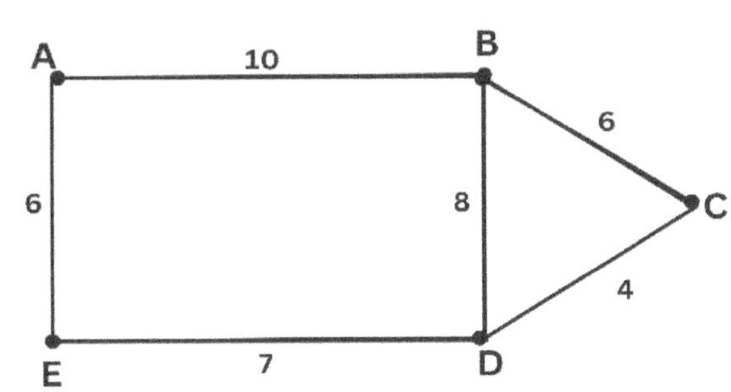

(b) What is an AVL Tree? Discuss the mechanism of the following rotations used in AVL tree: 10
   (i) LL
   (ii) LR
   (iii) RR
   (iv) RL

MCS – 021
M. C. A. (REVISED)/B. C. A. (REVISED)
(MCA/BCA)

Chapter 19: Term-End Examination, June- 2023

MCS-021: DATA AND FILE STRUCTURES

Time: 3 Hours
Maximum Marks: 100
Weightage: 75%

Note: (i) Question No. 1 is compulsory.
(ii) Answer any three Questions from the rest.
(iii) All algorithms should be written near to C language.

1. (a) Write an algorithm for the multiplication of two n×n matrices. Calculate both time and space complexity for this algorithm. 10

(b) What is a sparse matrix? Write an algorithm that accepts a 6×5 sparse matrix and outputs the 3-tuple representation of the matrix. 10

(c) Write an algorithm for array implementation of a linked list. 10

(d) What is binary search? Write an algorithm for binary search and find its complexity. 10

2. (a) What is a Splay Tree? Explain how it is different from a binary tree. 10

(b) Traverse the following binary tree in Pre-order and In-order: 10

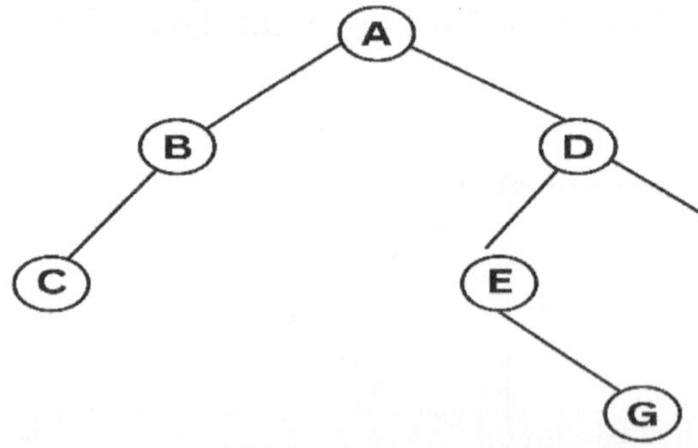

3. (a) Explain Quick sort algorithm. Sort the following set of data using this algorithm. Show intermediate steps of sorting: 20, 6, 8, 19, 36, 4, 28, 50 10

(b) What is Indexed Sequential File Organization? How is it different from direct file organization? Explain. 10

4. (a) What is a spanning tree? What are its applications? Write Kruskal's algorithm to find the minimum cost spanning tree and explain it in terms of its complexity. 10

(b) Define AVL tree. Write any two applications of AVL tree. 10

5. (a) Write algorithms for the following: 10

(i) To create a doubly linked list.

(ii) To delete an element from a doubly linked list.

(b) What is a stack? Explain PUSH and POP operations of a stack with the help of algorithms for each operation. 10

MCS – 021
M. C. A. (REVISED)/B. C. A. (REVISED)
(MCA/BCA)

Chapter 20: Term-End Examination, December- 2023

MCS-021: DATA AND FILE STRUCTURES

Time: 3 Hours
Maximum Marks: 100
Weightage: 75%

Note: (i) Question No. 1 is compulsory.
(ii) Answer any three Questions from the rest.
(iii) All algorithms should be written near to C language.

1. (a) What is an algorithm? What is the complexity of an algorithm? Explain the trade-off between space and time complexity with the help of an example. 8

(b) Write an algorithm for the following: 10
(i) Insert an element at the end of a linked list
(ii) Delete an element from a linked list

(c) What is a circular queue? Explain how it can be implemented using arrays. 10

(d) Write and explain Prim's algorithm for finding Minimum Cost Spanning Tree (MCST). 12

2. (a) Write an algorithm for insertion sort. Write the step-by-step working of this algorithm for sorting the following list of data: 8, 10, 25, 8, 16, 27, 2, 45 10

(b) Draw an AVL tree by inserting the following elements one by one: 10
8, 13, 27, 9, 12, 15, 10, 35, 25

3. (a) Write an algorithm for adding two polynomials. 10

(b) Explain indexed sequential file organization with the help of an example. 10

4. (a) Traverse the following binary tree in pre-order and post-order: 10

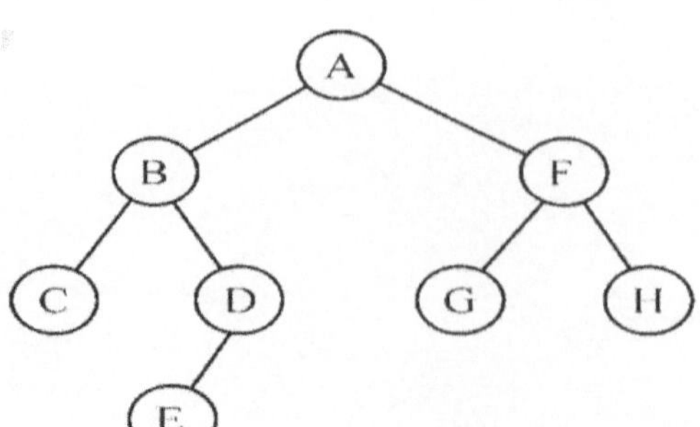

(b) What is a Red-Black tree? Explain the properties of a Red-Black tree. Explain how a node is inserted in a Red-Black tree. 10

5. (a) Write and explain an algorithm for binary search. Also, explain the applications of binary search. 10

(b) What is Breadth First Search (BFS)? Explain the difference between BFS and Depth First Search (DFS). 10

9 789369 728015

Printed at Repro India Ltd.